EXPLORING WORLD CULTURES

Israel

Alicia Z. Klepeis

Cavendish Square
New York

Published in 2017 by Cavendish Square Publishing, LLC
243 5th Avenue, Suite 136, New York, NY 10016

Website: cavendishsq.com

This publication represents the opinions and views of the author based on his or her personal experience, knowledge, and research. The information in this book serves as a general guide only. The author and publisher have used their best efforts in preparing this book and disclaim liability rising directly or indirectly from the use and application of this book.

CPSIA Compliance Information: Batch #CW17CSQ

All websites were available and accurate when this book was sent to press.

Cataloging-in-Publication Data

Names: Klepeis, Alicia Z.
Title: Israel / Alicia Z. Klepeis.
Description: New York : Cavendish Square Publishing, 2017. | Series: Exploring World Cultures | Includes index. Identifiers: ISBN 9781502621542 (pbk.) | ISBN 9781502621610 (library bound) | ISBN 9781502621559 (6 pack) | ISBN 9781502621566 (ebook)
Subjects: LCSH: Israel--Juvenile literature.
Classification: LCC DS126.5 K55 2017 | DDC 956.94--dc23

Editorial Director: David McNamara
Editor: Kristen Susienka
Copy Editor: Rebecca Rohan
Associate Art Director: Amy Greenan
Designer: Joseph Macri
Production Coordinator: Karol Szymczuk
Photo Research: J8 Media

The photographs in this book are used by permission and through the courtesy of: Cover Robert Landau/Corbis/Getty Images; p. 5 Ilan Shacham/Moment/Getty Images; p. 6 Peter Hermes Furian/Shutterstock.com; p. 7 O M/Shutterstock.com; p. 8 Aleksandar Todorovic/Shutterstock.com; p. 9 Rolls Press/Popperfoto/Getty Images; p. 10 GALI TIBBON/AFP/Getty Images; p. 12 filippo giuliani/Shutterstock.com; p. 14 Arava Power Company/File:APC.Ketura.jpg/Wikimedia Commons; p. 15 Daviddarom/File:Gulf of Eilat (Red Sea) coral reefs.jpg/Wikimedia Commons; p. 16 Roman Yanushevsky/Shutterstock.com; p. 18 Roman Yanushevsky/Shutterstock.com; p. 19 Opachevsky Irina/Shutterstock.com; p. 20 Boris-B/Shutterstock.com; p. 21 S1001/Shutterstock.com; p. 22 Mattes/File:Israel Batch 2 (318).JPG/Wikimedia Commons; p. 24 Rob Stothard/Getty Images; p. 26 irisphoto1/Shutterstock.com; p. 27 ChameleonsEye/Shutterstock.com; p. 28 Leonid S. Shtandel/Shutterstock.com; p. 29 Walter Bibikow/AWL Images/Getty Images.

Printed in the United States of America

Contents

Israel is a country in the Middle East. It has many special traditions and celebrations. People have lived there for thousands of years. Different groups, like the Romans and Egyptians, once ruled what is now Israel. Today, Israel is a free country. Its government is a **democracy**.

People in Israel have many kinds of jobs. Some work in schools or banks. Others carve diamonds or make high-tech products. People also grow food on farms.

There are lots of beautiful places to visit in Israel. It has deserts, beaches, mountains, and valleys. Families often enjoy camping as a way to see nature. Visitors come from around the world to tour Israel's amazing historical and religious sites. People also visit its cities, especially Jerusalem.

Israelis value the arts, music, and literature. They also enjoy playing sports and eating good food. Israel is a fascinating country to explore.

A group of tents and mountain bikes sits beneath a beautiful sunset in Israel's Negev desert.

Israel is about the size of the state of New Jersey. It covers 8,630 square miles (22,352 square kilometers). It borders Egypt, Jordan, Lebanon, Syria, and the Palestinian Authority. The Mediterranean Sea borders Israel to the west.

Red dots mark the biggest cities on this map of Israel.

Israel has many different landscapes. Galilee is a high, flat plateau in northern Israel. It has some of the nation's best farmland. The Jordan River flows through northern Israel. It empties into the Dead Sea. Hills and

Israel's Animals and Plants

Israel is home to many different plants and animals. Acacia trees, date palms, and poppies grow here. Ibex and eagles live here too.

mountains run down Israel's center. The Negev Desert is in southern Israel. This desert only gets about 1 inch (2.54 centimeters) of rain each year!

Southern and eastern Israel have hot, dry climates. Other parts of Israel have more **temperate** climates.

FACT!

The Dead Sea is so salty that people float without any effort.

Two young women float easily on the Dead Sea.

History

People have lived in what is now Israel for thousands of years. Historians don't know much about the earliest people in Israel. The Canaanites lived in the area as far back as 2000 BCE, but they

Hisham's Palace, built in the eighth century CE near Jericho, sees many tourists each year.

were conquered by the Israelites.

Over its history, many powers ruled Israel. The Egyptians, Babylonians, Greeks, and Romans are some examples. In the 1500s, this region became part of the Ottoman Empire. Then, in the early 1900s, **Arabs** living here fought against

Ottoman rule. In 1920, Great Britain and France took over. They established Palestine. Jews and Arabs fought here. In 1948, the State of Israel was created. Today, the Palestinians and Israelis still fight. Peace seems hard to achieve.

FACT!

Many Jews moved to Israel during World War II.

David Ben-Gurion

David Ben-Gurion was the first prime minster of the State of Israel. He is known as the "father of the nation."

David Ben-Gurion in 1970

Israel is divided into six districts called *mehozot*. Israel's capital is Jerusalem. Its government has three parts:

German politician Norbert Lammert (*top left*) speaks at a special session at the Knesset in June 2015.

1) legislative: In Israel, this is known as the Knesset. People in the Knesset write new laws. Israel's Knesset is made up of a single house. It has 120 members.

FACT!

Israeli citizens can vote when they are eighteen years old.

2) judicial: The courts make up this part of Israel's government. Unlike most nations, Israel does not have a constitution. It has Basic Laws.

3) executive: The president, the prime minister, and the **cabinet** ministers make up this part of the government. The prime minister runs the government. The president is the head of state.

Military Service

Almost all Israeli men and women are required to serve in the military, starting at age eighteen. Men must serve for thirty-two months. Women must serve for twenty-four months.

The Economy

Israel has one of the bigger economies in the Middle East. It trades mostly with Europe and North America. Its currency is often called the shekel.

Lettuce leaves grow on a farm using a drip irrigation system.

About 80 percent of Israelis have service jobs. Some work in banks, schools, and hotels. Others have jobs in museums, stores, and hospitals. Over three million tourists visit Israel each year.

Israeli workers are creative. People working in technology designed excellent water-saving

Some Israelis live on special farms called *kibbutzim*. All people in a kibbutz share everything from work to food to decision-making.

devices and invented new **irrigation** techniques. Factories in Israel make many different products, like communications equipment and medical electronics.

Farmers in Israel grow many crops. Citrus fruits, vegetables, and cotton are a few. The country also produces dairy products and wine.

FACT!

Gottex is a famous swimsuit company founded in Israel. People wear Gottex bathing suits on beaches around the globe.

Israel's animals, plants, and people need clean water and air to live. Some places in Israel do not have these things. Cities like Jerusalem, Tel Aviv, and Haifa suffer from air pollution. Traffic and factories send bad chemicals into the air and make it dirty.

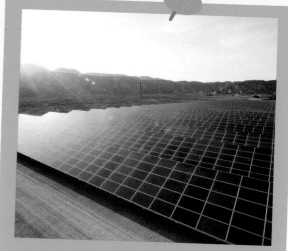

This large solar field is located on Kibbutz Ketura, Israel.

Many rivers in Israel are polluted. Lots of wells for drinking water are not clean either.

FACT!

Many cases of childhood asthma in Israel are linked to air pollution.

Many different animals and plants live in Israel. Pelicans, scorpions, and fennec foxes are just a few. Some animals are now threatened. Highways, housing, and other developments are replacing their habitats.

Israel gets nearly all of its energy from fossil fuels like oil. However, the country is starting to use other energy sources like solar power.

Israel's Coral Reef

Many people visit Israel's beautiful coral reef in Eilat. But numerous corals here face extinction because of changes in the water quality.

Eilat's coral reef is in the Red Sea.

The People Today

More than eight million people live in Israel. It is one of the world's most crowded countries. Israel's biggest city is Tel Aviv-Yafo. It is home to over 3.6 million people.

A bubble parade takes place in Tel Aviv's Habima Square.

The Haredim

The Haredim are a group of very religious Jews in Israel. They wear traditional clothing and live differently from most Israelis.

Around two-thirds of Israel's population was born in Israel. Other Israelis have come from over one hundred different countries. In the 1980s, many Jews from Ethiopia moved to Israel. Many Jews from Russia settled here in the 1990s.

FACT!

Israel has a special law called the Law of Return. It says that every Jewish person has the right to settle in Israel.

About 75 percent of Israelis are Jewish. Most other people in Israel are of Arab ancestry. Israeli Arabs often live in northern Israel. They also live in the cities of Yafo, Haifa, and Acre.

Lifestyle

People in Israel live in different ways. More than 90 percent of Israelis live in cities and towns. Because space is limited, city-dwellers often live in apartments rather than houses.

A street car waits at the Mount Herzl stop in Jerusalem.

Some people in the city drive cars to work. Others take buses or rail systems. Many urban families have computers, TVs, and cell phones.

FACT!

The unemployment rate for Arab men in Israel is twice as high as for Jewish men.

People living in the countryside often lead slower-paced lives. Some raise animals and grow crops. Others work on farms that produce items like olive oil. Some Israelis work in ski resorts or national parks.

This area of terraced farming is located on a kibbutz in Israel's Golan Heights area.

Many Israeli women today work outside of the home. They have jobs as doctors, teachers, bankers, businesspeople, and more.

Conflict in Israel

Israelis and Palestinians have fought for decades. This has been an especially big problem in areas like the West Bank and the Gaza Strip.

Religion

Religion is very important to many Israeli people. About 75 percent of Israel's people are Jewish. But only about 20 percent follow the rules of the Jewish religion very carefully. For instance,

This McDonald's in Tel Aviv serves kosher food.

they only eat food that is **kosher**.

Jews celebrate several holidays during the year. Yom Kippur is a holy day where Jewish people pray for forgiveness. Passover celebrates the time in Jewish history when the Jews left Egypt to escape from slavery.

FACT!

Jerusalem is considered a holy city by Jews, Christians, and Muslims.

Many people come to Jerusalem's Western Wall for Shabbat prayer.

About 17 percent of Israel's people are Muslim. They worship in buildings called mosques. Other religious groups live in Israel too. The Druze follow a religion that is like Islam. The Druze communities keep mostly to themselves.

Shabbat

Shabbat is a day of rest for traditional Jewish families. It begins at dusk on Friday and continues until Saturday evening. In many places in Israel, everything shuts down on Shabbat.

Language

Hebrew is the most commonly spoken language in Israel. Until the 1800s, Hebrew was a language only used for prayer and religious studies. Today, it is an official language of Israel. The country's government uses Hebrew.

These signs in Haifa are written in Hebrew, Arabic, and English.

Not everyone speaks Hebrew, though. Most Israeli Arabs speak Arabic at home. Arabic is also an official language in Israel. People have moved to Israel from around the world and speak many different languages. About one million people speak Russian as their first language. Israel's government provides documents to people in a variety of languages.

Unlike English, Hebrew is written from right to left. The Hebrew alphabet has twenty-two letters.

Israelis usually learn to speak more than one language. Schools in Israel teach children Hebrew, Arabic, and English.

Learn a Little Hebrew

If you want to say "hello," say "shalom" (pronounced sha-LOHM). In Hebrew, "hello" looks like this: שלום

People in Israel create different kinds of art. Some artists paint or sculpt. Their works are shown in galleries and museums around the world. Other Israelis make films. Both Jerusalem and Haifa host international film festivals each year.

Music festivals are celebrated in Israel every year.

Israel also celebrates music. Classical music is popular here, but Israeli musicians also make other music. Many people enjoy new jazz, rock, and pop music.

Israel has festivals all year round. Most of the country's public holidays are related to Judaism. Rosh Hashanah is the Jewish New Year. It takes place in the fall. People in Israel celebrate Independence Day in the spring. This holiday marks the day when David Ben-Gurion declared Israel's independence in 1948. Israelis celebrate with dancing, barbecues, and fireworks.

Calendars

There are two different calendars in Israel: a Hebrew calendar and a Western calendar. The Hebrew year is eleven days shorter than the Western calendar.

Fun and Play

There are lots of ways to have fun in Israel. Many Israelis enjoy sports. Soccer and basketball are the country's most popular sports. Just like in the United States, Israel has professional basketball and soccer leagues.

Two scuba divers inspect the coral as they explore in the Red Sea.

 FACT!

Israel has 115 national parks and 380 nature reserves.

Kids in Israel enjoy playing sports from a young age. Judo and swimming are well liked. In wintertime, people ski at Mount Hermon in northern Israel. In the summer, people go scuba diving in the Mediterranean Sea or the Red Sea.

Lots of people in Israel like to play games. *Matkot* is a game played on the beach. Players use wooden paddles and a small ball. They try to hit the ball to one another for as long as they can.

Israeli men play *matkot* on a beach in Ashkelon.

Maccabiah Games

Every four years Israel hosts the Maccabiah Games. Jewish athletes from around the world compete in many sports like tennis and track and field.

Food

People in Israel eat many kinds of food. A popular Jewish dish is **matzo** ball soup. Hummus is also popular. It is a thick spread made from ground chickpeas,

Matzo ball soup with flatbread

sesame seeds, olive oil, garlic, and lemon juice. Many Israelis like falafel, made of spiced chickpeas.

Israelis eat lots of fruits and vegetables. Olives, apricots, and grapes are popular here. People in Israel often drink coffee and tea. Fruit shakes and lemonade are also favorite beverages.

Food Shopping

Some Israelis shop at big supermarkets. Others shop at local markets like Jerusalem's covered market.

A covered market in Jerusalem's Old City

Some Israelis follow strict rules about eating certain foods. Some Jewish people cannot mix dairy products with meat. They don't eat shellfish or pork. Muslim people are not supposed to eat pork or drink alcohol.

FACT!

In Israel, it's common to eat the main meal of the day at lunchtime. Children come home from school for lunch.

Glossary

Arab   A person originally from the Arabian peninsula and neighboring territories.

cabinet   A group of advisors who help the political head of a government.

democracy   A system of government in which leaders are chosen by the people.

irrigation   The process of supplying water to crops or land, often by means of channels.

kosher   Referring to food that satisfies the requirements of Jewish law.

matzo   Unleavened bread that is eaten at Passover.

temperate   Having a climate that is normally mild without extremely cold or hot temperatures.

Find Out More

Books

Edgar, Sherra. *Israel*. North Mankato, MN:

    Child's World, 2015.

Gregory, Joy. *Israel*. Exploring Countries.

    New York: AV2 by Weigl, 2014.

Website

TIME: A Day in the Life: Israel

http://timeforkids.com/destination/israel/day-in-life

Video

Video Travel Diary: A Road Trip Across Israel

http://www.theatlantic.com/video/index/247334/

video-travel-diary-a-road-trip-across-israel

This wordless video by Matthew Brown has

spectacular photography of many sites in Israel.

31

Index

About the Author

Alicia Z. Klepeis began her career at the National Geographic Society. She is the author of many kids' books, including *The World's Strangest Foods*, *Bizarre Things We've Called Medicine*, *Francisco's Kites*, and *From Pizza to Pisa*. She lives with her family in upstate New York.